First World War
and Army of Occupation
War Diary
France, Belgium and Germany

50 DIVISION
149 Infantry Brigade
Royal Dublin Fusiliers
2nd Battalion
1 June 1918 - 30 April 1919

WO95/2831/1

The Naval & Military Press Ltd
www.nmarchive.com
Published in association with The National Archives

Published by

The Naval & Military Press Ltd

Unit 10 Ridgewood Industrial Park,

Uckfield, East Sussex,

TN22 5QE England

Tel: +44 (0) 1825 749494

www.naval-military-press.com

www.nmarchive.com

This diary has been reprinted in facsimile from the original. Any imperfections are inevitably reproduced and the quality may fall short of modern type and cartographic standards.

© **Crown Copyright**
Images reproduced by permission of The National Archives, London, England, 2015.

Contents

Document type	Place/Title	Date From	Date To
Heading	WO95/2831 2nd Battalion Royal Dublin Fusiliers Jun 1918-Apr 1919		
Heading	50th Division 149th Infy Bde 2nd Bn Roy. Dublin Fusrs. June 1918-Apr 1919. Absorbed 7 Battalion 6.6.18 From 16 Div 46 Bde		
Heading	War Diary 2. R. Dub Fus. 1 June 18 to 30 June 18. Volume 46		
War Diary		01/06/1918	14/06/1918
War Diary	Val de Lumbres.	15/06/1918	16/06/1918
War Diary	Rouxmesnil	17/06/1918	26/06/1918
War Diary	Martineguse	27/06/1918	30/06/1918
Miscellaneous	50th. Division. G.X. 19/12.	16/11/1918	16/11/1918
Miscellaneous	The Royal Dublin Fusiliers		
Miscellaneous	Prices of the 7th Bn. "The Royal Dublin Fusiliers"	12/07/1918	12/07/1918
Miscellaneous		12/07/1918	12/07/1918
Heading	War Diary. 2nd. Bn. Royal Dublin Fusiliers. from:- 1st July 1918 To:- 31st July 1918 Volume No. 48.		
War Diary	Martin Eglise.	01/07/1918	31/07/1918
Miscellaneous	Strength Return. 2nd. Bn. Royal Dublin Fusiliers.	12/07/1918	12/07/1918
Miscellaneous	149th Inf. Bde. N.B.C.37/1.	20/07/1918	20/07/1918
Miscellaneous	2nd Battalion. Royal Dublin Fusiliers.	11/07/1918	11/07/1918
Heading	War Diary 2nd Bn Royal Dublin Fusiliers From 1st to 31st August 1918 Vol. XLIX.		
War Diary	Martin Eglise.	01/08/1918	28/08/1918
Heading	War Diary 2 R. Dub. Fus from 1 Sept 1918 to 30 Sept. 1918. Volume No 50		
War Diary	Martin Eglise.	01/09/1918	15/09/1918
War Diary	Iverny	16/09/1918	26/09/1918
War Diary	Behancourt.	27/09/1918	28/09/1918
War Diary	Nurlu.	28/09/1918	31/10/1918
Miscellaneous		17/10/1918	17/10/1918
Miscellaneous	Company Commander Points.		
Map	Mesplaux		
Map	Trenches & Information Corrected To 14:10:18		
Heading	War Diary of 2 Bn. Royal Dublin Fusiliers from 1 Nov. 1918 to 30 Nov 1918 Vol 52		
War Diary	Sheet 57.B. L.20. Pommereuil	01/11/1918	03/11/1918
War Diary	Sheet 57.A Fontaine Au Bois	04/11/1918	04/11/1918
War Diary	Sheet 57.A. Les Etoquies.	04/11/1918	05/11/1918
War Diary	Sheet 57.A. Leval.	06/11/1918	06/11/1918
War Diary	Sheet 57.A. St. Remy Chaussee	07/11/1918	07/11/1918
War Diary	Dourlers	08/11/1918	08/11/1918
War Diary	Floursies	09/11/1918	30/11/1918
Miscellaneous	Appendix To War Diary November 1918		
Miscellaneous	Officers 2nd Battalion the Royal Dublin Fusiliers	11/07/1918	11/07/1918
Heading	War Diary of 2nd Bn Royal Dublin Fusiliers from 1 December 1918 to 31 December 1918. Vol No 53		
War Diary	Baslieu	01/12/1918	04/12/1918
War Diary	Monceau St Waast	05/12/1918	18/12/1918
War Diary	Le. Quesnoy	19/12/1918	31/12/1918

Heading	War Diary of 2nd Battalion the Royal Dublin Fusiliers from 1st January 1919 To 31st January 1919. Vol. No 54.		
War Diary	Le Quesnoy	01/01/1919	31/01/1919
Heading	War Diary of 2 Batt. The Royal Dublin Fusrs from 1st February 1919 to 28th February 1919. Vol No. 54		
War Diary	Le Quesnoy	01/02/1919	28/02/1919
Heading	War Diary Of 2nd Battalion the Royal Dublin Fusiliers for the Month of March 1919 Volume Number 55		
War Diary	Le. Quesnoy	01/03/1919	31/03/1919
Heading	War Diary of 2nd Battalion the Royal. Dublin Fusiliers from 1st April 1919 to 30th April 1919 Volume No 57.		
War Diary	Le Quesnoy	01/04/1919	30/04/1919

① WO95/2831

2nd Battalion Royal Dublin Fusiliers

Jun 1918 – Apr 1919

50TH DIVISION
149TH INFY BDE

2ND BN ROY. DUBLIN FUSRS.
JUNE J̶L̶Y̶ 1918 - APR 1919.

ABSORBED 7 BATTALION 6.6.18

From 16 DIV 48 BDE

Confidential

War Diary 2．R．Brothers．

1 June '18 to 30 June '18.

Volume 46

Army Form C. 2118.

WAR DIARY
INTELLIGENCE SUMMARY.
(Erase heading not required.)

3rd Bn Royal Dublin Fusiliers

Instructions regarding War Diaries and Intelligence Summaries are contained in F. S. Regs., Part II. and the Staff Manual respectively. Title pages will be prepared in manuscript.

Place	Date	Hour	Summary of Events and Information	Remarks and references to Appendices
	1 June 18		The Battalion (Training Staff) now belong to the 9th Corps Bn. 31st Div.	
	2 June 18		The day was devoted to cleaning up the camp. The Commanding Officer received a letter from Brigadier General Carl, D.S.O. Comg 46th Inf Bde. (16th Irish) Divn. of which the following is a copy:- "I feel sure you know much of that the loss of your Battalion - for two and a half years now I have had to watch in silent wonder my Bde. Concerned and I am very proud I have had the honour of having them in my Bgde. so long. No troops could have served better and I am indeed grateful to them for all the good work they have done for me. I shall be most indebted to hear how you get on. The best of good luck to you and the Battalion." Sd/Frank Ramsay Chief of Staff. Inspection parade. Ordinary games and inspections.	
	3 June 18 4 June 18 5 June 18 6 June 18		The 7th Bn. detained at ARCQUES (ST. OMER) and marched into Camp at 11 p.m. The Bn. left England on 10 July 1915, and landed at Gallipoli, Serbia Macedonia and Palestine. It embarked at ALEXANDRIA, EGYPT on 23rd May 1918 as disembarked at MARSEILLES on June 1st 1918. Strength on arrival 33 officers 814 other ranks. of the Battalion consisting of 7 officers and the rate forms the Training Staff of the 7th Batn; the remainder were the day absorbed into the 2nd Battalion. Practically all the officers and men are subject to attacks of malaria contracted on the STRUMA. Reorganisation commenced.	
	7 June 18 8 June 18		The Battalion marched out of Camp complete with transport, and proceeded to Vat. DE LIEPRES leaving the Training Staff behind. Dinners were served from the cookers at WIZERNES. 112 N.C.O. and men fell out on the line of march, of these 20 were picked up & carried to Hospital.	

Army Form C. 2118.

WAR DIARY
or
INTELLIGENCE SUMMARY.
(Erase heading not required.)

Instructions regarding War Diaries and Intelligence Summaries are contained in F. S. Regs., Part II. and the Staff Manual respectively. Title pages will be prepared in manuscript.

Place	Date	Hour	Summary of Events and Information	Remarks and references to Appendices
	9th June 1918.		Lieut. W.S. Maitland and 38 Other Ranks, Transport personnel left at DESVRES to hand over 2nd Bn Transport & and instruct Transport personnel of 3rd Bn. 59th Regt. of United States Infantry in Transport Duties, rejoined the Battalion with 30 Other Ranks reinforcements.	
	10th June 1918.		Training.	
	11th June 1918.		Training.	
	12th June 1918.		Training.	
	13th June 1918.		Major General Campbell Commanding 31st Division lectured to all officers of the Brigade on Discipline and Esprit de Corps.	
	14th June 1918.		Training.	
			Commanding Officer, Adjt. and Coy Commanders proceeded by Bus to WALTON CAPPEL and reconnoitered the Army line of trenches near HAZEBROUCK with a view to possible occupation.	
			Orders received for the Brigade to move to STAPES.	
WAL de LUMBRES	15th June 1918		The 3rd Royal Norfolk force entrained for STAPES at 9am. Light duties on morning of 15th. The 2nd Royal Munsters two hrs and 3rd Royal Dublin Fus being ordered to proceed at 3 P.M. at 7 P.m. the Orders for the Dublins and Munsters was cancelled.	
	16th June 1918		Church Service in afternoon. Recreational games and platoon the shooting competition at 10.35 P.M. while still at the ranges orders were received to march to WIZERNES - 6 miles and entrain with full transport for back area at 6 P.m.	
			The Battalion proceeded by Infantry and Bus arriving about 5 P.m. On arrival Transport to Battalion entrained at 10 P.M.	
ROUXMESNIL	17th June 1918		Battalion arrived at ROUXMESNIL at 3 P.m. detrained and occupied the Detail Camp with the Norfolks. Tea and various details. Battalion under orders of N.Y.C.	
	18th June 1918.		Battalion placed on five of commandeering rations. Capt. Guard up.	
	19th June 1918.		Battalion inspected by F.R.C.L. Valcympleton G.H.O. Genl. J. Adair to Battalion, daily orders.	
	20th June 1918.		Usual training parades. Tea Bathing for the troops day at Dieppe - 5Klos away. Boys to take Lookers and Lane Dinkers on the Shore and play games before returning to Camp	
	21st June 1918.		Usual parades. Capt. A.S. Oglines Joins the Battalion.	
	22nd June 1918.		Usual parades.	
	23rd June 1918.		Usual parades.	
	24th June 1918.		Usual parades. Divine parades commence.	

Army Form C. 2118.

WAR DIARY
or
INTELLIGENCE SUMMARY.
(Erase heading not required.)

Instructions regarding War Diaries and Intelligence Summaries are contained in F. S. Regs., Part II. and the Staff Manual respectively. Title pages will be prepared in manuscript.

Place	Date	Hour	Summary of Events and Information	Remarks and references to Appendices
ROUX MESNIL	25 June 26 June		Usual Parade. New camping ground marked out. 'A' Coy to proceed to new camp between the Road & farque and the village of MARTIN EGLISE to pitch camp for the Battalion.	
MARTIN EGLISE	27 June 28 June 29 June		'B' & 'D' Coys & Bn. HQ. proceed to new Camp leaving 'C' Coy to clear up old Camp and forward stores to 'C' Coy follow from old Camp Building up of heaps carried out. Several required to affects with Braziers are erected to cartepathere camps.	
	30 June		Usual Parade and working Parties to Camps from allotments of four per day was Paraded to the Station. The first batch embarked at BOULOGNE on 23.0.	

J Brady Capt.

Lieut Colonel
Comdg 2nd Batn. Royal Dublin Fusrs

CONFIDENTIAL.

50th. Division.
G.X. 19/12.

D.A.G.
   G.H.Q., 3rd. Echelon,
      B A S E.

      Reference your letter No. 140/452 dated 26th. September 1918.

      Herewith War Diary of the 2nd. Bn. Royal Dublin Fusiliers for the month of June, 1918.

16th. November 1918.
                          Major-General,
                       Commanding 50th. Division.

Précis of the Battn.
"The Royal Dublin Fusiliers."

The Battn. embarked from Southampton on the 22nd August 1914 and landed at Boulogne on the 23.8.14 with the 4th Divn. Took part in the Battle of LE CATEAU on the 26.8.14 and was very badly cut up. The remnants of two Companies that were cut off from the Battn. wandered about behind the German lines & eventually found their way to DUNKIRQUE and from thence to England.
During the end of August & the beginning of Sepr. the Battn. took part in the Retreat from Mons and the Battles of the MARNE and the AISNE.
On Oct. 14. 1914 they were relieved by the French troops and later took part in the Battle of MEETEREN: and also took part in the actions around BAILEUL – ARMENTIÈRES and HOUPLINES. The winter of 1914 – 1915 was spent at PLOEGSTRAAT. In April 1915 the 4th Divn. were taken out for a ten days

were suddenly flung into the 2nd Battle of Ypres on the 25.4.15.
The Bn lost 17 officers and 300 men on that day.
On the 8th May Bn lost 300 men (while holding line around POTIZE and on the 24 May Bn was gassed at ST JULIEN — only 1 Officer and 35 other Ranks returned.
On 6 July the Bn took part in the attack on PILKEN RIDGE and lost 300 men. The Bn was then withdrawn to HOUTER KERQU for rest and at the end of July relieved the French down South in front of SERRE. The winter of 15.15 - 16 was spent in the vicinity of BEAUMONT-HAMEL. The Bn then took part in the SOMME offensive on the 1st July 1916 — casualties 20 officers — 400 oRanks.
August and Sept were spent up round YPRES then Bn was ordered SOUTH to take part again in the SOMME Battle attacks and took the village E. of LE TRANSLOY on the 28th Oct 1916 — only 3 officers and 60 oRanks survived.
At the end of Nov. 1916 Bn joined the 16th Irish Divn at front of BAILLEUL

Précis of the 7th Bn.
"The Royal Dublin Fusiliers"

The Battn. was raised at the latter end of 1914 and the early months of 1915. It was chiefly composed of men for Dublin but prior to embarkation for overseas it received drafts for the "D.C.L.I." — "the West Kents" and the "Wiltshire Regt." — the West Surrey's — "R.E." & R.F.A. They embarked from Plymouth on July 10th 1915 and landed at SUVLA BAY on August 6. 1915. Here they took part in the landing and suffered heavy casualties in Officers and men. The Bn. left SUVLA on the Sept. 18. 1915 300 strong.
They landed in SALONIKA on Oct. 8. 1915 and then commenced trekking for SERVIA which they reached on Nov. 13. 1915. The Bn. took part in the retreat from SERVIA Dec. 12. 1915 suffering very few casualties about 35 prisoners and wounded. On Dec. 22. 1915 the Battn. landed at LANGAZA in GREECE. The winter of 1915/1916 was spent in digging trenches and awaiting a Bulgarian offensive

and the winter of 1916-1917 was spent in
vicinity of KEMMEL HILL. and
On 6 June 1917 Bn took part in attack
on the MESSINES RIDGE — Casualties
Slight — then later in the attacks
W of YPRES on July 31st and August
16th — in the latter attack only
6 officers & 200 ranks returned
At the beginning of Sept 1917 Bn went
South to hold the line in front of
BAPAUME and took part in the
CAMBRAI offensive on the 23 Nov —
Casualties Slight.
The winter of 1917-1918 was spent in the
vicinity of PERONNE and Bn was
in the front line trenches in the EPEHY-
RONSSOY sector when the German
offensive commenced on 21st March 1918.
Bn took part in the retreat of the 5th Army
and was relieved on the 4 April —
Strength 3 officers and 30 other ranks.
Bn left the 16th Divn about April 1918
and went to the 31st Divn where it was
amalgamated with the 7th .....
on the

[signature] Capt.
I.R. Dub Fus.

12/7/18

The Bn. landed at ALTIAC near SALONICA at the end of July 1916 and carried out a programme of training until July 1916. At the end of July 1916 Bn. went to CETHANA and trained until Oct. 1916 when they went up to the STRUMA PLAIN.
They took part in the minor actions on the STRUMA during 1917.
In Sept 1917 they left SALONICA for EGYPT arriving at the latter place on 20 Sept. 1917.
The Bn. did its Share in the advance from GAZA and held the line opposite the TURKS until APRIL 1918.
Left Egypt on 26 May 1918 and landed at MARSEILLES on 1st June 1918.
Amalgamated with the 2nd Bn. on the 6th June 1918

[signature]
Capt.
2 R. Dub. Fus.

12/7/1918.

(6392) Wt. W6192/P875 1,500,000 4/18 McA & W Ltd (E 2815) Forms W3091/4. Army Form W.3091.

Cover for Documents.

Confidential

Nature of Enclosures.

WAR DIARY

2nd. Bn. ROYAL DUBLIN FUSILIERS.

From :- 1st July 1918
To :- 31st July 1918

VOLUME No. 48.

Notes, or Letters written.

Army Form C. 2118

WAR DIARY
or
INTELLIGENCE SUMMARY
(Erase heading not required.)

Instructions regarding War Diaries and Intelligence Summaries are contained in F.S. Regs., Part II. and the Staff Manual respectively. Title Pages will be prepared in manuscript.

Place	Date	Hour	Summary of Events and Information	Remarks and references to Appendices
MARTIN EGLISE.	1st July 18.		Training Parades carried out, also some working parties in the New Camps.	
	2nd	"	Training Parades, and working parties.	
	3rd	"	Training parades, and working parties.	
	4th	"	Working parties.	
	5th	"	The Commanding Officer inspected the kits of the Battalion at 9 a.m.	
	6th	"	Working parties.	
	7th	"	Church Parades. Lieut. D.C.A. Shephard, Lieut. C.W.Kidson, 2/Lt. S.A. Morris and 2/Lieut. S. Byrne, joined from the Base.	
	8th	"	Working parties. Sea water and fresh water Bathing. Lieut. G.R. Attwood, 4th R.I.Fus., rejoined for duty.	
	9th	"	Training parades. The Commanding Officer and 14 other Officers were conducted round Ammunition dump, Bakery and Docks by Colonel Cutlack.	
	10th	"	Sergeant-Major's Parade at 7.15. a.m. Usual Parades from 9.30 to 12.30. p.m.	
	11th	"	Adjutant's Parade 8.30. a.m. to 9.30. a.m. Usual training parade from 10.a.m. to 12.30.p.m.	
	12th	"	Commanding Officer's Parade 8.30 a.m. to 9.30. a.m.	
	13th	"	The Battalion Paraded at 11 a.m. for inspection by Brigadier-General P.M. Robinson, C.M.G., and Major-General H.C.Jackson, D.S.O., Commanding 50th Division. The Commanding Officer and Adjutant met the Brigadier and Brigade Major near the Base Supply Depot and were shewn the field in which the Battalion would rest and also its position in line for the review on the PLAGE for 'FRANCE DAY'.	
	14th	"	The Battalion Paraded at 7.10. a.m.: 15 Officers, 416 other ranks - and marched off to DIEPPE. The troops in the Garrison were drawn up in line with backs to the sea :- A squadron of Cavalry on the right - then 3rd Bn. Royal Fusiliers, 1st Bn. K.O.Y.L.I., 2nd Bn. Rl.Muns. Fus. and the 2nd Bn. Rl. Dub. Fus. The massed bands of the 50th Division and Belgian Buglers supplied the music. Major-General H.C. Jackson, D.S.O., Commanding 50th Division took the 'GENERAL SALUTE' in line. The troops then marched past in column and returned in quarter column. Column of route was formed and troops marched through the streets on their way back to camp. Nearing camp General Sir H.S. Rawlinson, Bt., G.C.V.O.; K.C.B., K.C.M.G., complimented Lieut-Colonel Weldon on the smart appearance of the Battalion. Draft of 30 from Calais.	
	15th	"	The Battalion moved from No 11 Camp to No 5 Camp where 149th Brigade is being encamped.	
	16th	"	Training Parades. Lieut-Colonel.(T/Brig-Genl.) P.M. Robinson, C.M.G., R.W.Kent Regt. Comdg.	

(Over)

- 1 -

WAR DIARY
or
INTELLIGENCE SUMMARY

(Erase heading not required.)

Army Form C. 2118

- 2 -

Place	Date	Hour	Summary of Events and Information	Remarks and references to Appendices
MARTIN EGLISE.	16th July	18.	(Continued:- 149th Infantry Brigade made the acquaintance of various Officers and inspected their Army Books 439 (Records of Service).	
	17th July	18.	The Brigadier inspected the Battalion on Parade.	
	18th	"	Training Parade and work on Camp. Captain C.G. Carruthers, M.C. joined the Battalion.	
	19th	"	Training Parade and work in Camp. Captain A. Browne, 2nd Garr. Bn. Cheshire Regt. and 60 men of 7th Bn. from Egypt joined the Battalion. The Brigadier, Brigade Major and Staff Captain spent the morning in Camp.	
	20th	"	Training Parades. Brigadier and Brigade Major in Camp at 12 noon. Conference of C.O's held at Division.	
	21st	"	Church Parades. 'Digging in' of tents commenced, as a protection against Aircraft Bombardments.	
	22nd	"	Training Parades. Commanding Officer attends conference - Brigadier and Divl. Cdr present in R.E. Camp. Draft of 35 O.R. arrived.	
	23rd	"	Battalion on work in Camp Area. Brigadier's lecture to Officers on the War.	
	24th	"	Training Parades. Brigadier and Brigade Major in Camp 9.15 a.m.	
	25th	"	Training Parades.	
	26th	"	Battalion finds working parties. No training - Lieut. J. N. Barry arrived.	
	27th	"	Training Parades. G.O.C. and Brigade Major in Camp in forenoon.	
	28th	"	Church parades.	
	29th	"	Working parties. No training. G.O.C. in Camp at 11 a.m. Lieut. G.P.O(Sulli)van joined and took over duties of Battalion Signalling Officer. Divl. Commander explained Battalion, Company and Platoon Organization to C.O., Coy. Commanders in School Room at 5 p.m.	
	30th	"	Training Parades. 4 Platoons working on Bayonet Assault Course. G.O.C. lectured to all available Officers at 2 p.m.	
	31st	"	Training Parades. G.O.C. in Camp at 10.45. a.m. - saw men firing on 30^X range.	

1st August, 1918.

Lieut-Colonel,
Commanding 2nd Battn. Royal Dublin Fusiliers.

STRENGTH RETURN.

2nd. Bn. Royal Dublin Fusiliers.

	Officers	O.R.
Present with Battalion.	31	588
On Command.	—	4
Leave to United Kingdom.	7	80
Absentees.		2
In Hospital and not evacuated.	4	8
Total Effective Strength.	42	682.

360 Other Ranks have been admitted to Hospital, evacuated, and struck off Effective Strength since the landing in France of the 7th. Bn. Royal Dublin Fusiliers. on 1st June 18

8 Officers were admitted during this period, 2 of whom have been invalided to England.

M Weldon Lieut.Col.,
Comdg. 2nd. Bn. Royal Dublin Fusiliers.

12/7/18.

C O N F I D E N T I A L

50th Division.

149th Inf.Bde.
N.B.C.37/1.

Herewith Battalions History and
Records as requested.

Abraham Clark Capt
for. Brigadier General,
Commanding 149th Infantry Bde.

20.7.18.

2nd Battalion. Royal Dublin Fusiliers.

Return of Leave for N.C.Os and men who have not had leave for one month and upwards.

```
Not had
leave for 1 month.                551.
Do for 2 months.                  495.
"    "   3    "                   485.
"    "   4    "                   473.
"    "   5    "                   462.
"    "   6    "                   448.
"    "   7    "                   433.
"    "   8    "                   423.
"    "   9    "                   403.
"    "  10    "                   365.
"    "  11    "                   312.
"    "  12 X  "                   302.
"    "  13    "                   297.
"    "  14.   "                   291.
"    "  15.   "                   283.
"    "  16.   "                   258.
"    "  17.   "                   251.
"    "  18. X "                   219.
"    "  19.   "                   140.
"    "  20.   "                   133.
"    "  21.   "                   114.
"    "  22.   "                   106.
"    "  23.   "                   106.
"    "  24. X "                   106.
"    "  25.   "                   106.
"    "  26.   "                   106.
"    "  27.   "                   106.
"    "  28.   "                   105.
"    "  29.   "                   105.
"    "  30.   "                   .105.
"    "  31.   "                   105.
"    "  32.   "                   103.
"    "  33.   "                    25.
"    "  34.   "                    25.
"    "  35+36 "                   nil — (on leave now)
```

                                 Lieut-Colonel,
                      2nd Battn. Royal Dublin Fusiliers.

11th July, 1918.

Confidential

War Diary

2nd Bn Royal Dublin Fusiliers

From
1st to 31st August 1918

Vol. XLIX

Army Form C. 2118.

WAR DIARY
or
INTELLIGENCE SUMMARY.
(Erase heading not required.)

Instructions regarding War Diaries and Intelligence Summaries are contained in F. S. Regs., Part II. and the Staff Manual respectively. Title pages will be prepared in manuscript.

Place	Date	Hour	Summary of Events and Information	Remarks and references to Appendices
MARTIN EGLISE.	1st Aug.1918.		Lecture by G.O.C. to all Officers at 2 p.m.	
	2nd	"	Training. "C" & "D" Coys. attended Divl.Gas Hut to have S.B.Rs tested.	
	3rd	"	Training. Lt.O'Neill,Sgt.McGhee,L/Sgt.Elston & 10 men re-joined from 1st Battalion.	
	4th	"	Church Parade.	
	5th	"	Training Demonstration of "Coy. in attack" carried out by a Coy. of Scottish Horse. Demonstration of Coy. in attack by "C" Coy.(interrupted by rain).	
	6th	"	Brigade Working Day. Range Practices. Demonstration follows. Lecture by Col.Levey.G.H.Q. Tg. Staff on "Training Methods". Headquarter Coy. formed. Conference with G.O.C.	
	7th	"	Training. "A" and "B" Coys. tested at Gas Hut.	
	8th	"	Brigade Work Day. C.O8s conference at Brigade. Adjutants conference with G.S.O.1. Divn. and Brigade Majors at 5.30 p.m.	
	9th	"	Divisional Operations.	
	10th	"	Church Parades.	
	11th	"	Brigade Work Day. Reconnaissance of ground for Bde.Operations. Cross Country Race by 139 men of Battalion.	
	12th	"	Brigade Work Day.	
	13th	"	Route March. 8.a.m. to 12. noon in Drill Order. Lecture by Col.James on Aeroplanes. Lieut. Attwood proceeds to England on 6 months tour of duty.	
	14th	"	Brigade Operations in afternoon. Lieut. Beaumont to England on 6 mths. tour of duty.	
	15th	"	Brigade Work Day.	
	16th	"	Bombing ground and short range used all day. (BOMMERY) Training.	
	17th	"	Church Parades. Divl. Horse Show. Battn.won Inf. Transport Group Cup and 100 francs obtaining % marks	
	18th	"	Brigade Work Day.	
	19th	"	Training during day. Battn.Night Operations. Lt-Col.K.C.Weldon,DSO, assumed Command of 149th Bde. during absence on leave of Brig-Genl. Major L.C.Byrne,MC, assumed Command of Battalion.	
	20th	"	Battn. returned off night Operations at 6 a.m. "ALL CLEAR" 10.20. a.m.	
	21st	"	Brigade Work Day. Hostile Aircraft sounded at 9.45 a.m.	
	22nd	"	Battalion route march. 3 hours in full marching order. 1 men fell out.	
	23rd	"	Training.	
	24th	"	Church Parades.	
	25th	"	Battalion Training.	
	26th	"	Battalion Route March. Parade 6 a.m. March to Berneval. Musk.and Bathing return to Camp 3 p.m.	
	27th	"	Aug. 29th. Training. Aug.30th. Training. Aug.31st. Bde.Work Parties.	
	28th	"	Bde.Work Parties.	

J Brady Capt for Major,
Commanding 2nd Bn. The Royal Dublin Fusiliers

Confidential

WAR DIARY.

2 R. DUB. FUS.

from 1 Sept 1918
to 30 Sept. 1918.

Volume No 50

Army Form C. 2118.

WAR DIARY
or
INTELLIGENCE SUMMARY.
(Erase heading not required.)

Instructions regarding War Diaries and Intelligence Summaries are contained in F. S. Regs., Part II. and the Staff Manual respectively. Title pages will be prepared in manuscript.

Place	Date	Hour	Summary of Events and Information	Remarks and references to Appendices
MARTIN EGLISE.	1st Sept 1918	—	Church Parades.	
"	2nd	—	Training and Hot Bath. Lecture on recent fighting by R.A. Officer.	
"	3rd	—	Training and Brigade work parties – Smoke Barrage demonstration.	
"	4th	—	Divisional Route March – 14 miles – No men fell out.	
"	5th	—	Training.	
"	6th	—	Divisional Horse Show 7am to 8pm. Dinners out.	
"	7th	—	Training.	
"	8th	—	Church Parades. Lecture by a Naval Officer on Anti-Submarine Campaign.	
"	9th	—	Bde. work parties. Lecture by Col. Campbell on the Bayonet. Lecture by Mr. Alex. Irvine on "War Aims".	
"	10th	—	Training – Divisional Sports.	
"	11th	—	Training.	
"	12th	—	Divisional operations.	
"	13th	—	Training.	
"	14th	—	Training and preparing to move by Rail.	
"	15th	—	Bn. less 'C' Coy entrained at ARQUES at 10 p.m. for BOQUEMAISON	
IVERNEY.	16th	—	Bn. less 'C' Coy arrived at BOQUEMAISON at 7.15 a.m. Breakfasted and marched to billets at IVERNEY – 4 kilos.	
"	17th	—	'C' Coy – (Less D.C.A. Shepard, left at ARQUES) left at ARQUES to load Bde. Baggage rejoined Bn. at 3.15 a.m.	
"	18th	—	Training.	
"	19th	—	Brigade Field Day.	
"	20th	—	Battalion Route March. Lieut. J.N. Bowrn, posted to 11th Bn. Northumberland Fus. and struck off strength of this Battalion. Lieut. W.C. Conarchy proceeded to U.K. for 6 months duty and is struck off the strength of this Battalion. Draft of 24 O.Rs joined from Base.	
"	21st	—	Brigade Field Day.	
"	22nd	—	Church Parades. G.O.C. inspected drafts at 11 a.m. Lecture on "Tanks" by Lt. Col. McKern, D.S.O.; to all officers and Platoon Sergeants.	
"	23rd	—	Battn. Route march with tactical exercises.	
"	24th	—	Training.	
"	25th	—	Training.	
"	26th	—	The Battn. embussed at 10 a.m. and proceeded BEHANCOURT.	
BEHANCOURT.	27th	—	Training.	
"	28th	—	The Battalion re-organised in accordance with O.B. 1919 as follows:-	

Fighting Portion – Officers 24. Other Ranks – 612.
Administrative Portion – Officers 2. Other Ranks – 91.
Battle Surplus. Officers 9. Other Ranks – 181.
Fighting and Administrative Portions under Command of Major L.C. Byrne M.C., embussed at

(P.T.O)

Army Form C. 2118.

WAR DIARY
or
INTELLIGENCE SUMMARY.

(Erase heading not required.)

Instructions regarding War Diaries and Intelligence Summaries are contained in F. S. Regs., Part II. and the Staff Manual respectively. Title pages will be prepared in manuscript.

Place	Date	Hour	Summary of Events and Information	Remarks and references to Appendices
RLV.	28th Sept. 1918.	1.30 p.m.	BEHANCOURT at 1.30. p.m. and proceeded to NURLU arriving at 9.30. p.m. The Battalion bivouacked here for the night. The Battalion Surplus marched to POULAINVILLE arriving in Billets at 8. p.m.	69
	29th		The Battalion moved into huts in NURLU.	
	30th		The Battalion being warned for immediate action, all Battle Stores were completed — fighting order adopted and all ranks stood by ready to proceed to the line at one hour's notice.	

Whure
Major for
Lieut-Colonel,
Commanding 2nd Bn. Royal Dublin Fusiliers

18th October, 1918.

WAR DIARY
or
INTELLIGENCE SUMMARY.

(Erase heading not required.)

ORDERLY ROOM
1 NOV 1918
2nd BATTN. ROYAL DUBLIN FUSRS.
No. ......

Place	Date	Hour	Summary of Events and Information	Remarks and references to Appendices
	1st Oct 1918	1	Battn at NURLU standing by awaiting orders.	
		2	Commanding Officers went up to reconnoitre at 9 am. Battn moved at 3 pm to TETARD WOOD near EPEHY and relieves 3rd & 5th Canadian Inf Btn. KNOLL TR during night. Battn in reserve. Enemy retaliated gas shelling.	
		3	D Coy attached MAILLINCOURT Post. 2 in Comd. Officer & 1 O.R. missing. Patrol to Batt and Batn I Scout SGT found HINDENBURG LINE unoccupied. With Australian Batn the moved to LONE TREE TR.	
		4		
		5	Attack at 5.45 am. "C" & "D" Coy advanced on HINDENBURG LINE and captured MALAUMCOURT. F.P. PULTER did very fine work & Sergeant Bay wounded.	
		6	Order to QUINDAM PAX MILL and HARGIVAL FM at dawn. My coy to delay & came up to Co. with assistance 9th RTS. Officers were killed enough ahead to knock the later Hans GERMAN positions to TR TERRIERE. 33rd Mks between Battn. We worked our to venly. B LONG TREETR for info. Battn any machine transport brought up & the points. Battn pushed to LA PANNERIE went to report to 10th Bn. At 6pm night forward track there are adages in high ground - life front. There Quarry. 5 other wounded Battn. Ho moved to QUARRY and suffered heavily road in front. At 1.30 am "C" Coy supported by "D" Coy attempted to take TICKETS by MG fire and the captured by gap replies in mine crater was to enemy. Major & Co Realese advanced wounded in enemy before dark. Co. North reconnoitred to Ke. It was stronger hand.	

WAR DIARY
or
INTELLIGENCE SUMMARY.
(Erase heading not required.)

Army Form C. 2118.

Instructions regarding War Diaries and Intelligence Summaries are contained in F. S. Regs., Part II. and the Staff Manual respectively. Title pages will be prepared in manuscript.

ORDERLY ROOM
F 1 NOV 1918
2ND BATT N. ROYAL FUSRS.

Place	Date	Hour	Summary of Events and Information	Remarks and references to Appendices
	8-6-c 1916		continued to cut wire. he was afterwards killed. At 10 p.m. the 157 Bde relieved the 149 Bde who went into support behind TROIS MILE QUARRY.	
	9	1 am	the 157 Bde attacked & captured VILLERS FM. at 5/10 unsuccessful attack on VILLERS OUTREAUX. 8am 4th Army went forward. At 119 Bde were in reserve to its being afternoon Bath moved into GUISANCOURT to be in touch. Afew Hols were dropped in the vicinity.	
	10	4pm	Batt. marched back to ETRICOS in C.O.L.	
	11		Bath. went to ETMAPETZ then marched to TMAROIS spent night in billets.	
	12		Paraded with brigade by Am. of TMAROIS. No parades.	
	13	3pm	Batt. moved to HONNECHY Capt Barlow Neill and D. Bonelli and Pierre wounded. the former died from his injuries.	
	14		known Services Parade. Batt. stood another's employers to show regions cemeteries near SENLE & east of St. BENIN.	
	15		training Batt. painted numerous employers charges of to attack eastern part of BENIN in fully places	
	16		OC. Reps reconnoitred positions at St BENIN prior to moving the 2nd Brigade to attach.	
	17		Battn. supplied billets at HONNECHY. At 6 30 am. "B" Coy lifts serpent attacked at 6.30 am bath crossed to SELLE Run tony bridge was at war for the attack left pinned bnd train and Coy	

(A5004) Wt. W2711/M2-31 750,000 5/17 Sch. 52 Forms/C2118/14

WAR DIARY
or
INTELLIGENCE SUMMARY.
(Erase heading not required.)

Instructions regarding War Diaries and Intelligence Summaries are contained in F.S. Regs., Part II. and the Staff Manual respectively. Title pages will be prepared in manuscript.

ORDERLY ROOM
Army Form C. 2118.
1 NOV 1918
2nd BATTN. ROYAL DUBLIN FUSRS.

Place	Date	Hour	Summary of Events and Information	Remarks and references to Appendices
			Heavy M.G. fire on which A Coy suffered heavily. B. Kildare and Lackey killed.	
		06.30	Tank and some SH moving N along W. [illegible] By 8th Batn in [illegible] in [illegible] to [illegible] on left but movement on left.	
		8.30	Patrols sent out a Cpl & one of "D" Coy did not return	
		8.45	Info taken from prisoners firing from [illegible] operation and came to report	
		10.15	Roylis report counter attack developing on left. Did not materialize	
		11.30	Some Royls and KRR withdrawn to railway	
		12.35	Patrol Sno reports on R's active line with Americans on right KRR & Royls on left	
		4.00	Batt'n pivot with Scottish thro' for R's active line	
		4.25	R's at Q.6 & 8.5 (57B) in our on right	
		7.45	M.O. moved to S. BENIN	
		7.55	Batt'n dugin 200 - 300 ahead of [illegible] and Rue.	
		8.30	Bn HQ in tunnel at position reached at 17.55. Dublin F.m. pure high by [illegible]	
18.10.18		00.30	Coy readers in DUBLIN on right northway of bombardment	
		01.50	Coys forced to but withdraw at 05.30 owing to bombardment	
		05.30	Bn in [illegible] with enemy barrage & frauze reported	
		11.40	Left Coy from on to Rsl'ns on same as the 25 Bn have for to work	
		14.00	Relieved by other enemy M.Gs on [illegible] Q.6.a with few M.G. on right.	

WAR DIARY
or
INTELLIGENCE SUMMARY.
(Erase heading not required.)

Instructions regarding War Diaries and Intelligence Summaries are contained in F.S. Regs., Part II. and the Staff Manual respectively. Title pages will be prepared in manuscript.

Army Form C. 2118.

Place	Date	Hour	Summary of Events and Information	Remarks and references to Appendices
19/10/8		16.10	Hours afraid to repulse enemy and to cut continue to turn in rife	
		21.00	American on rife Batt ordered to withdraw to B 30 & 37 (5/6) exposed to Mchy by at 10.00 on 19th	
		10.50	Batt withdrew from line. heavy gun by cookers Casualties 2 officers + 35 OR. killed, three officers + 150 wounded Cpl Grace +3 men killed afterwards with 35 missing	
	20.10.18		Carriages to Caudry	
	21.10.18		Re-organisation parade — ordered up the line Pentr.	
	22.10.18		16.00 CO advance Brigade	
	23.10.18		Dig off + baths	
	24.10.18			
	25.10.18	15	Lt. Col K Weldon K.T.O. assumes temporary command 5th Bn Bn Major	
	26.10.18		Training at MARETZ	
	27.10.18		Machine gun & Lewis gun fighting	
	28.10.18		Bombing work	
	29.10.18		move of cataphault in REUMONT	
	30.10.15		move from REUMONT to billets in LE CATEAU	
	31.10.18		Training in LE CATEAU	

Oct.17th.
12-30.a.m. Battalion left HONNECHY.

3.a.m. Arrived at Assembly point at 3.a.m. Q.27.A.5.6 and was in touch with Scottish Horse at once. Formed up in trenches 1,2,3,4- order-

5-30.a.m. No.1.Company went over - platoons at 50 yards in file. 2 Officers and 20 casualties passing through Enemy's barrage up to River.

6.15.a.m. Crossed River without difficulty- floating tree- men fell in.

6.30.a.m. Lined embankment-1,2,3,4 to collect Battalion- very misty- Platoon from No.1.Company sent up to find K.R.R. Found them this side of Y Nullah in 29.A. where they had been held up.

7.20.a.m. Came back with this information. Smoke and fog made it impossible to see. Much machine Gunning.

7.30.a.m. Ordered to push on in support of 151 on to Red dotted Line- to support 60th and K.O.Y.L.I.- No advance to RED LINE until in touch with Americans on right and Dublins on left.
All four Companies in line and in diamond formation. Depth of each Company 150 - 200 yards.
Breadth 100 yards and 50 yards between Companies- this on account of the mist.

8.5.a.m. Reached Red dotted line. No Americans on Right- no sign of Dublins on left - 4th.K.R.R. on road.
No.1.Coy. formed defensive flank.
No.2.Coy. clear of K.R.R.
No.s 3 & 4 Coys intermingled - 4th K.R.R. having had very heavy casualties.

Germans shelling road and machine gun fire in enfilade.

Americans 1200 yards away with gap of 1000 yards x 1200

No.1.Company formed defensive flank right hand man being about Q.24.C.5.3.

8.20.a.m. No.2.Company sent 2 platoons on to crest in advance and 2 platoons on road itself half way to copse.
No.3.Coy. ditto - assisted K.R.R. and found Coy of K.R.R. on the left

9.a.m. No.4.Company went straight through and to within 20 yards of Q FARM - with assistance of Tank No.43 advanced to FARM- took 33 prisoners and S.M.- occupied small trench (30 men) 2/Lieut. Rogers and S.M.Sargeant-

No.3 Company extended to left to assist K.O.Y.L.I.

8.30.a.m. Americans back- and did not move from Railway Embankment till 11.a.m.

11.a.m. No.4.Company withdrew about 11.a.m.-owing to heavy shell fire and machine gun fire from counter attack S.M. killed

page 2-

and 2/Lieut Rogers left at FARM- Bosche advance to within 100-200 yards to road

11.a.m. C.O. of 4th K.R.R. decided to withdraw and form defensive flank.

Few Americans came up to Red dotted Line- about one hundred.

11.15.a.m.(?) O.C.No.3-Coy ordered withdrawal to Red dotted Line-

Both Battalions became mixed.

K.R.R. formed defensive flank on left, as K.O.Y.L.I. had disappeared. Royal Fusiliers withdrew to conform to line of 60th, 300 yards S.W. of Red dotted Line.

Platoon Commander of No.2.Company reported German Field Battery coming into action about 600 yards to immediate front about Q.24.A.7.6., firing over open sights- opened on Battery with Lewis Guns.

12 noon to 1.p.m. No.1.Company indicated fire to aeroplane who fetched six other scouts, who machine gunned FARM and counter attacking points of enemy for 40 minutes.
No.1.Company fired on advancing Germans (10) and drove them back.

At 11.30.a.m. C.O. saw Brig. Gen. Rollo who stated 150th Infy. Brigade were pushing forward through Red dotted to Red Line at 12.30.p.m.
3rd. R.F. to form a right defensive flank in case Americans didnt push on.

12.30.p.m. Attack cancelled about 12.30.p.m.

(a) The withdrawal from QUENNELET FARM was ordered on account of the Company being isolated and the heavy Artillery and Machine Gun Fire.

(b) The withdrawal of the three remaining Companies and the 60th was ordered by Capt. Gordon because both flanks were exposed and a better field of fire was obtained.
No.1.Company maintained a post 50 yards N.N.E. of FARM to watch N.E. down the Nullah- No Americans were up to the right flank at this time.

1.30.- 2.p.m. A final position was occupied facing N. and N.E. running from the S.of FARM in Q.29.B.2.8- round the FARM and thence parallel with N.arm of Y Nullah- down to junction of Y Nullah in Q.29.A. 3095- thence Line was continued N.W. by the 4th K.R.R.

The Americans were in touch on our right. No.1.Coy having a platoon in liasion with them about 100 yds S. of FARM in Q.29.B.2.8-
The situation remained the same until 6.30.p.m. when the 7th Wilts had orders to push through to the Red dotted line and to consolidate there. 3rd. R.F. were ordered to consolidate in depth behind the Wilts, which was done.

Each Company was ordered to send an officer's patrol to get in touch with the 7th Wilts and be ready to support that Battalion.

17th/18th.

The night passed fairly quietly.
At 2.30.a.m. 150 Infy Brigade Order No.   was received ordering attack on RED LINE at 0530 a.m. 18th Oct.
Orders were issued to Companies to support the Wilts 300 yards in rear- 4 Companies in Line in diamond formation.
Battalion was formed into 3 Companies- No.4-Coy being absorbed into No.3-
The Battalion formed up as ordered and by moving out of Y Nullah escaped German barrage.

5.a.m.

Battalion Headquarters moved to Q.29.A.7.1. and remained in trench with the C.O. 7th Wilts throughout the day.

6-30.a.m.

No.1.Company held up by machine Gun fire near QUENNELET GRANGE FARM, the left platoon being about 50 yards from FARM- this fire came from the ridge N.E. of it.
No.2-Company went through and mopped the Farm this having been ommitted by the 7th Wilts.
No.3-Company with three platoons passed Farm on right.
7th Wilts were now reported to be withdrawing; this was stopped and Wilts advanced as far as road in Q.18.D. where they started to dig in.
The Germans were not properly mopped up in QUENNELET GRANGE FARM.
Both Wilts and Americans appeared to run into the barrage.

7-30.& 8.a.m.

The Wilts started to consolidate E. of road in Q.18-D. supported by 3rd. R.F. in Q.18-B. and D.

11.a.m.

The Wilts were held up by a machine gun in the enclosures in Q.18.B. and D.; this was finally cleared up by the 25th Division.

3-p.m.

The Battalion consolidated on a line facing E. of Q.18.B. 2.2. to Q.24.B.3.8. into a S.P. round N.E. side of QUENNELET GRANGE FARM.
2 Coys in Line and one Coy in S.P.
Apparently the 7th Wilts mistook the final objective or were unable to get on to the Red Line owing to enemy fire.

Neither the 4th K.R.R. nor the Americans captured LA ROUX FARM; This Farm held a commanding position and was not captured until about 2-p.m. by the Americans.

Company Commanders Points.

1. Barrage too quick to allow mopping up of Farms.

2. Units must be definitely earmarked to mop up strong localities.

3. Fog was so dense on both days during the first three hours that it was difficult to control troops or spot German Machine Guns.
   In such weather a later hours such as 9.a.m. or 10.a.m. would have been better.

4. Inter-communication must be maintained by means of Officers Patrols by units.

5. In view of the strength of the Battalion the frontage given them was much too great.

MESPLAUX

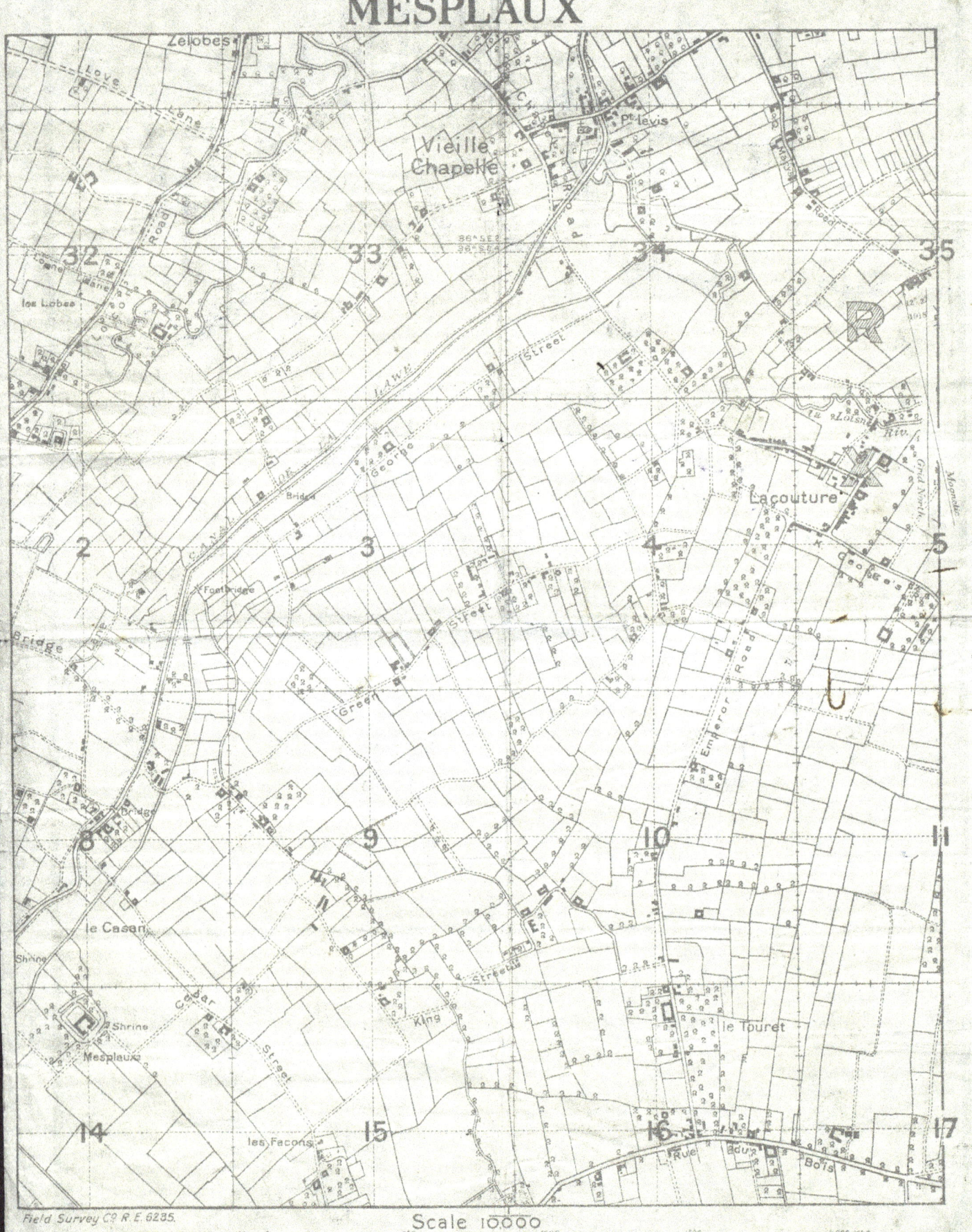

Scale 10,000

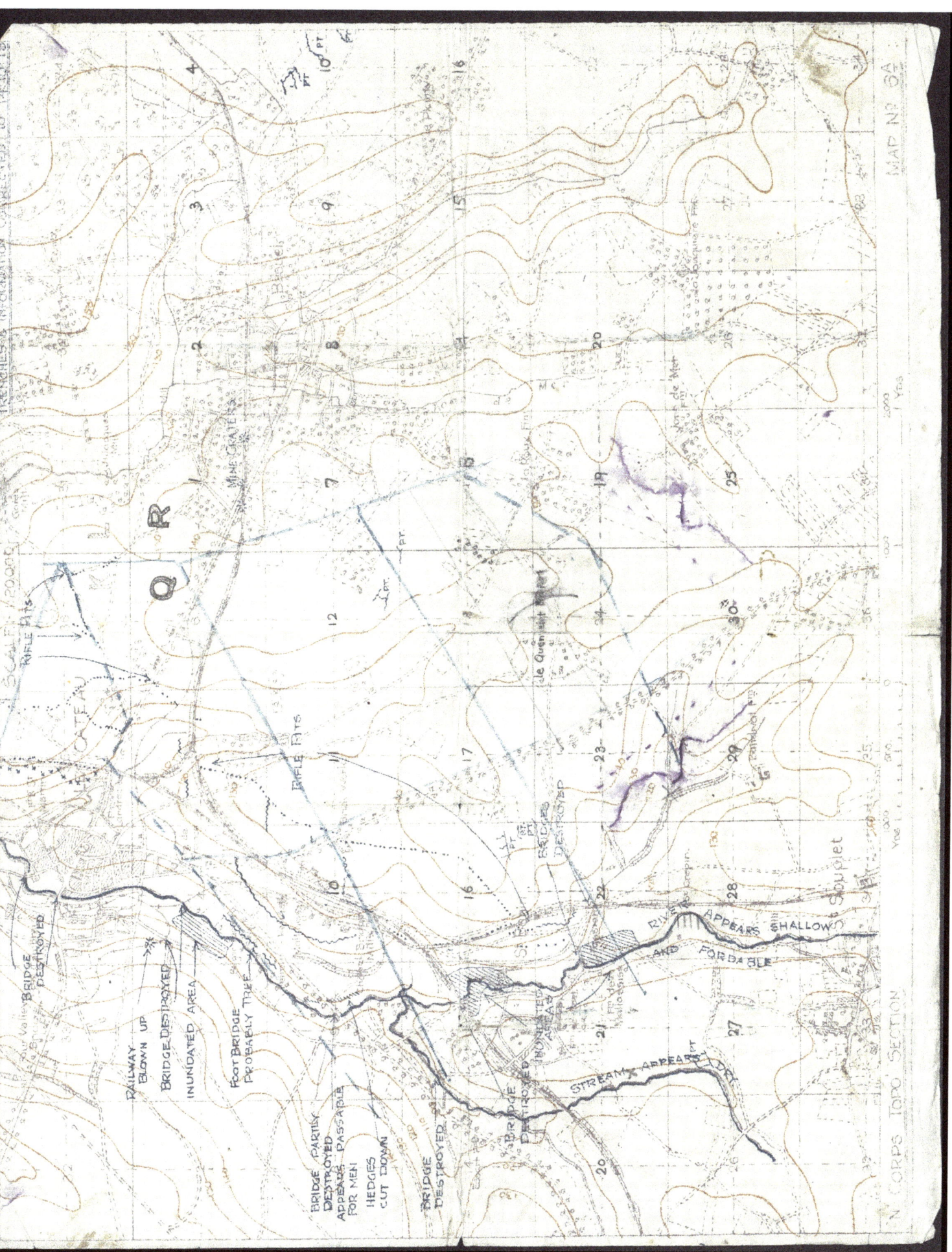

Army Form W.3091.

Cover for Documents.

Nature of Enclosures.

War Diary of
2 Bn. Royal Dublin Fusiliers
from
1 Nov. 1918 to 30 Nov. 1918

Vol. 52.

Notes, or Letters written.

Army Form C. 2118.

WAR DIARY
INTELLIGENCE SUMMARY.
(Erase heading not required.)

2 B Royal Dublin Fusiliers

Instructions regarding War Diaries and Intelligence Summaries are contained in F. S. Regs., Part II. and the Staff Manual respectively. Title pages will be prepared in manuscript.

Place	Date	Hour	Summary of Events and Information	Remarks and references to Appendices
Sheet 57.B. L.20. POMMEREUIL	1-11-18		Battalion in bivouacks at POMMEREUIL.	
	2-11-18		do — do — slight bombardment of bivouacks with high bursting Shrapnel causing the following casualties:— 2/Lieut. J.C. Hewitt wounded 1.O.R. Killed and 1 O.R. Wounded.	
Sheet 57.A. FONTAINE AU BOIS	3-11-18 4-11-18		The Battalion moved at 3.a.m. to take part in a Major operation to be carried out on a front of 50 miles, the Brigade objective being the Southern part of the FORET LE NORMAL. The Battalion was in Brigade Reserve and moved forward from FONTAINE AU BOIS at Zero hour (0615 hours) 800" behind the attacking Battalions. The Battalion almost immediately came under a heavy barrage and suffered heavy casualties. When the attacking Battalions had reached their objective in the front, this Battalion was ordered to go forward & take and hold the important spur in H.13.a and H.7.c which overlooks LANDRECIES and enfilades the Canal SUMBRE both N. & S. The spur was attacked by D. Company under Capt. J.N. Barry and about 10 men of "C" Coy. under 2/Lieut. P.A. Morris. and was reported taken at 12.30 hours. A Battery of enemy Field Guns attempting to come into action near the Canal bank was captured by these Coys. the Horses & Drivers being shot down and the Battery Commander captured.	

WAR DIARY
or
INTELLIGENCE SUMMARY.
(Erase heading not required.)

Army Form C. 2118.

Hour, Date, Place	Summary of Events and Information	Remarks and references to Appendices
Sheet 57.A. H-11-6. LES ETOQUIES.	In addition to this Battery, one other field gun and 23 H.2. howitzers were captured, also many L.Miss, and M.G's. The Battalion took the following prisoners :- 1 Officer and 20 Other Ranks and suffered the following Casualties:- 2/Lieut. H.J. McBrien Killed. 10 O.R's Killed. 2/Lieut. J.B. Crugg Wounded. 100 Other Ranks wounded, 2 & 3 wounded remaining at duty. Lieut. B.H. McElroy wounded, 3. G.R's missing Capt. A.M. Ewen & Lieut. L.I.H. Lloyd Blood wounded and remained at duty. Capt. E.J. Hamlet	
5-11-18.	The Battalion spent the day in billets. struck off strength on proceeding to U.K. for 6 months tour of duty. Authority 12/France/1937, M.S.I.R dated 13-8-17. Lieut. G.S. Harvie, 6th Bn. R. Dub. Fus., attached yth Bn. Suffolk Regt. joined for duty. Authy. G.B./2158/683A/(C) dated 24-10-18. The following Honours & Awards have been granted to N.C.O's and men of the Battalion for gallantry in the field near LE CATEAU :- No. 9441. Sergt. F. EGAN. BAR TO M.M. 28515 Pte W. MARCHANT. - do - 24242 Pte P. BOYCE. MILITARY MEDAL 24016 " J. REGAN. - do - 18244 " F. POWELL. - do - 29694 Cpl (A/Sgt.) J. BLADES. - do - 24684 Pte T. STOWE. - do - No. 12968. Pte P. HANLEY. MILITARY MEDAL 17298 A/Cpl P. MAHER. - do - 21584 Pte G. REID. - do - 29041 " F. ELSEY. - do - 24144 A/Cpl W. LUMBER. - do - 28514 " J. ROEBUCK. - do - 28514 Pte M. LIMES. - do - 15841 Cpl H. FORD. - do - 29150 " W. FRAY. - do - 43546 . A. MARSHALL. - do -	

WAR DIARY or INTELLIGENCE SUMMARY.

Army Form C. 2118.

(Erase heading not required.)

Hour, Date, Place	Summary of Events and Information	Remarks and references to Appendices
Sheet 57.A. LEVAL. 6-11-1918.	Lieut. Col. H.C. Welson. D.S.O. assumed took over command of the Battalion from Major J. LUKE near NOYELLES the Battalion being at the time in support of the Scottish Horse & Royal Fusiliers who were advancing on MONCEAU ST WAAST which was captured about 6. p.m. The Battalion moved into MONCEAU ST WAAST and billeted there in support to the Scottish Horse and Royal Fusiliers holding the line. The undermentioned N.C.O.'s and Men were awarded the MILITARY MEDAL for gallantry near LE CATEAU on 17th/18th October, 1918:- No. 28493. Corpl. J. HOOTEN. 28560. Lfcpl. F. SKINNER. (Died of Wounds) Y165. Pte. R. SNEDDON.	
Sheet 57.A. ST REMY CHAUSSEE 7-11-18 DOURLERS 8-11-18	The Battalion marched to ST. REMY CHAUSSEE in close support to the Scottish Horse & Royal Fusiliers. No action took place and the Brigade occupied billets for the night in the village. The Brigade moved by march route at 12 noon to DOURLERS with orders to pass through the outpost line on the MAUBEGE - AVESNES main road, held by the Division. On arrival at the outpost line at 2.30 p.m. the Battalion deployed through the K.R.R.C. & proceeded to attack enemy holding FLOURSIES. Major J. LUKE commanding firing line was soon wounded devolving under Capt. F.M. KIERNAN. Considerable opposition from M.G. nests was dealt with & the Battalion occupied the village. Owing to delayed action of troops on flanks, no captures were made. At 4. p.m an outpost line was thrown out beyond the village & defensive posts formed on the flanks.	

WAR DIARY or INTELLIGENCE SUMMARY

Army Form C. 2118.

Place	Date	Hour	Summary of Events and Information	Remarks and references to Appendices
FLOURSIES	9-11-18		pending arrival of units on flanks. Casualties:- Lieut. Perier - Killed. Lieut. Greaves and Major J. Locke wounded. 11 Other Ranks killed and 14 Wounded.	
	10-11-18		During the night Battalion Headquarters was moved to FLOURSIES and the units on flanks having come up Battalion advanced to edge of wood. 6.25 a.m. attack re-commenced. Battalion pushed through wood without opposition. Patrol pushed on to RUE HAUTE, orders having been received to hold the Forest, positions were taken up there.	
	11-11-18		Battalion remained in position. Coys being withdrawn to billets in FLOURSIES. Armistice signed at 11. a.m. "D" Coy. sent as outpost Coy to LA SAVAT.	
	12-11-18		Thanksgiving service for Division at Chateau grounds BOURLERS. Presentation of Medal Ribbons.	
	13-11-18		Companies re-organize & check stores.	
	14-11-18		Working party of 3 Officers, 200 Other Ranks proceeded to SARS POTERIES STATION to sort German shells. The Corps Commander, Gen. J.S.M. Morland, K.C.B., K.C.M.G., D.S.O., visited Col. Heldon.	
	15-11-18		Working party to SARS POTERIES.	
	16-11-18		— ditto —	
	17-11-18		Outpost withdrawn. "D" Coy remains at LA SAVAT. Working party to SARS POTERIES in afternoon. Divine Service in forenoon. Major L.C. BYRNE, D.S.O., M.C. rejoined off leave.	
	18-11-18		Coys. training forenoon. Games in afternoon.	

Army Form C. 2118.

WAR DIARY
INTELLIGENCE SUMMARY.
(Erase heading not required.)

Instructions regarding War Diaries and Intelligence Summaries are contained in F. S. Regs., Part II. and the Staff Manual respectively. Title pages will be prepared in manuscript.

Place	Date	Hour	Summary of Events and Information	Remarks and references to Appendices
FLOURSIES	19-11-18		Two Coys. on Salvage work. Two Coys. training.	
	20-11-18		"C" "D" Coys. Salvage work. "A" "B" moved to billets at BAS LIEU.	
	21-11-18		"A" "B" Coys. Salvage work. Remainder of Battalion moved to BAS LIEU at 10.a.m.	
	22-11-18		"C" "D" Coys. Salvage work. "A" "B" training. B. Genl. L.F. RENNIE visited Battn. 5.p.m.	
	23-11-18		"A" "B" Coys. Salvage work. "C" "D" training.	
	24-11-18		Church parade.	
	25-11-18		Battalion training by Coys. 9-11. Transport cleared dumps R.8 & 14.	
	26-11-18		Battalion training by Coys. 9.a.m. Names obtained for educational scheme.	
	27-11-18		Ceremonial drill 9.a.m. Classes of education & instruction formed. Divisional Commander, Major General H.E. Jackson D.S.O. inspected the Battalion billets, recreation rooms, cookers, transport etc.	
	28-11-18		Coy. at training. Educational classes under Rev. Father J.J. Delaney S.J. continued	
	29-11-18		Coy. at Drill parade. Educational classes continued. Medal ribbon presentation to Officers, N.C.O.'s and men at 3.20.p.m. by Divisional Commander.	
	30-11-18		Battalion paraded for Brigade practice parade in anticipation of the visit of the Majesty the King. Educational classes proceeded as usual. The following Honours & awards have been granted to N.C.O's & men of the Battalion for gallantry in the field on the 4th & 8th Nov. 1918:-	
			No 15834 Sergt. L. Perry. D.C.M	
			27480 W. Green. D.C.M.	
			12968 L/Cpl. G. Hanley. Bar to Military Medal	

Army Form C. 2118.

WAR DIARY
or
INTELLIGENCE SUMMARY.
(Erase heading not required.)

Places	Date	Hour	Summary of Events and Information	Remarks and references to Appendices
	30-11-18		No. 26941. A/Sgt. Singleton. G. — MILITARY MEDAL.	
			5698. Pte. Hardy. J. — do —	
			20522. " Dunn. J. — do —	
			30818. Sgt. Doyle. J. — do —	
			25590. " Blaholm. J. — do —	
			28740. Pte. Owen. J. — do —	
			21136. " Healy. L. — do —	
			19244. A/Sgt. Monaghue. J. — do —	
			24110. Sgt. Chambers. A. — do —	
			30108. " Mortimer. J. — do —	
			22219. Pte. Kenna. J. — do —	
			19879. " Killeen. J.M. — do —	
			16108. " Buggy — do —	
			28444. " Coffey. H. — do —	
			14245. " Gray. R. — do —	
			Effective strength Officers 34. O.Rs. 625.	
			Ration " " 29 " 637	

Brady,
Lieut. Colonel,
Comdg. 2nd Batt. Royal Dublin Fus.

WAR DIARY
or
INTELLIGENCE SUMMARY.
(Erase heading not required.)

Army Form C. 2118.

2 R Dublin

Place	Date	Hour	Summary of Events and Information	Remarks and references to Appendices
			APPENDIX TO WAR DIARY NOVEMBER 1918 Awards for gallantry in the field during operations of October and November were granted to the undermentioned of the Battalion :—	

M.C. 2/Lieut. J.E.H. Bouttle
 Capt. A.M. Crawford
 Lieut. D. Denton
 2/Lieut. J.B. Howell
 2/Lieut. C.W. Humphrey
 2/Lieut. W. Humphreys
 Lieut. D.R. Lambkin
 Lieut. L.J.K. Lloyd-Blood
 Lieut. G.H. McCray
 Lieut. L.A. Morris
 2/Lieut. L.P.G. Sullivan
 T/Lieut. J.V. Slopkin

BAR TO D.C.M.
6603 S/S. W. Cummins. D.C.M.

2ND BAR TO M.M.
11669 Pte Daly P. M.M.

BAR TO M.M.
9441 Sgt. J. Egan M.M.
12968 Pte D. Hanley M.M.
28515 Sgt H. Mordland M.M.

D.C.M.
24780 Sgt. W. Keen
24048 " J. Knightly
15834 " J. Perry

MILITARY MEDAL
24093 Sgt. Bass
29697 Pte Beacon
14920 L/Cpl Borland
24244 Sgt Boyne
6108 Pte Briggs
24110 Sgt Chambers
30590 " Chisholm
28444 Pte Clifton
19244 " Doyle
10314 L/C Quake
15841 Pte Elvey
29041 " Ford
15841 Cpl Gray
29050 A/Cpl Freeman
9223 Pte Freeman
28816 " Lice

MILITARY MEDAL
14245 Pte Earl
5698 " Haley
28493 Sgt Heard
20522 Pte Green
23219 Sgt Kenna
21046 Pte Kenna
19849 " McEwan
28513 " Lunes
24144 A/C Lunbon
14090 Sgt Mahon
14208 A/C Mahoney
43546 A/Cpl Manhurst
14116 Pte Manks
21136 " Mealey
19244 " Minogue
30108 Sgt Mahoney. D.C.M.
11341 Pte Murray. D.C.M.
11219 " Harrie
28444 A/Cpl Potock
28446 Pte Owen
18274 " Penneel
24016 " Regan
21584 " Reid
28544 " Rockwick

MILITARY MEDAL
26941 Pte Singleton
28560 A/Cpl Skinner
4645 Pte Smeeton
24654 " Stove
12968 " Stanley

Cpl E.H.

Officers 2nd Battalion The Royal Dublin Fusiliers

Rank	Name	Appointment	Date of 1st Commn	Date of Present Rank	Service in Present War From	To	Cause of Quitting	Courses Nature + place	Year	Honours & Mentions	Date of Embarkation or (L)ast Leave	Service in Ranks Years	Last Rank	Remarks
Lt-Col (Major)	R.C. Weldon D.S.O.	Commdg Bn	7.2.00	Major 1-9-15. T/Lt Col 1/7.10.16	Dec 15	present date	Still Serving	Hythe, though Dubl. Brig 1839 2nd Lieut. Regim Gym		19. S. G. Legion of Honour	(L) 10.4.18	✓	✓	Service continuous since Landing in France 7.9.16. Commanded 7th R.Innis Fus 7.10.16. 7.2.18 2R.D.F. 8.2.18
Major	S.G. de C. Weekes	Senior Major	.10.99	1.9.15.	12.8.14 23.1.18	25.4.15	Wounded	Hythe.		Mentioned in despatches. 1914	(4)	✓	✓	on leave
Major + QrMr	J. Burke M.C. D.C.M.	Q.M.	1-3-01.	8.12.14	22.8.14	—	Stillserving	Musketry M.G. Horsemanage 2 Rebrit'g 2 Roy Dub Fus	1888 1913-14	Mil Crdso 1916 3 mentions	(L) 28.6.18	19 7/12	R.S.M.	Twicewounded. Service in France continuous
Lieut (T/Capt)	J. Brady	a/Adjt.	11.2.15	29.6.15 (T/Capt.17.10.15)	4.8.14 23.12.14 5.15	23.12.14 7.16	from India Gassed Wounded.	Hythe. Musk.	6.0		(E)	17 8/12 Roy Dub Fus	C.S.M.	
Lieut	R.E. Bracken	Asst Adjt.	24-4-15	1.6.16.	12-15.	9.16.	Wounded	Bombing General	7.6.16. 7-16.		4.5.17	✓	✓	
Lieut	W.C. Conarchy	Scout Officer	1.7.17	1-1-17	1/16 Jan 17	11/17	for Commn	Scouting Snipg	4/18	leegazette 7-11-17.	(L) 9.7.18	2 6/12 6 Royal Highlanders	Sgt 6 Royal Highlanders	
Lieut	R.W.D'Barrey	Sig officer	26.3.15.	1.7.17.	Apl 15	—	✓	Sig. istanbula Bomb- in Sig. Egypt.	Aug 16 July 17 Feb 18		(L) 10.7.18	✓	✓	on leave
Lieut	G.R. Ottwood R.I.F.	R. Lewis officer	1-10-15.	1-7-17.	5-5-16 23.12.16	1-6.16	Wounded	L. Gunnery Dollymount Gas Stokes Gun	10/16 11/12/16 5/17	3 hatchets- L 16 Divn	(L) 7.7.18	✓	✓	
Lieut	W.S. Maitland M.C R.I. Rifles	Transport officer	20.5.15	1-7-17.	22.11.15 23.11.16	1-7-16	Wounded	Musketry Dollymount Platoon Cdr. Gas-	Sept 15 Jan 16 June 17	Mil. Cross 1-7-16.	(L) 7.7.18	7/12 20"Royal Fus	Cpl. 20"Royal Fus	
Captain	W.J. Craig A.A.M.C	M.O.	8.9.14.	24.1.17.	✓	✓	✓	—	—	✓	(L)	✓	✓	on leave
Lieut a/Capt	R.C. Byrne M.C.	O.C. A Coy	17.2.15	7.2.16 1.8.16	4.6.15 12.5.18	23.4.16 21.3.18	Wounded —	Coy Cdr, 1st P School	May 18	Mil Cross+ Bar 1917.	(E) 1.5.18	✓	✓	Acting 2 in Cd.
T/Capt	A.M. Ewen	2 i/cd A Coy	14.9.15.	4.10.17	10.7.15	15.6.18	Sick	Bombg. Salonika Gas General, Egypt.	11-16 6.17 3.3.18	—	(L) 12.4.17	12 month. 7R.D.F.	Cpl. 7R.D.F.	Hospl.

Officers. 2nd Battalion the Royal Dublin Fusiliers

Rank	Name	Appointment	Date of 1st Common	Date of Present Rank	Service in Present War From	To	Cause of Quitting	Courses Nature	Year	Honours & Mentions	Date of Embarkation	Service in Ranks Years	Last Rank	Remarks
Lieut a/Capt	H.G. Aylmer		15.1.15	1-1-17 (T. 8-8-16)	1-6-15 20-6-17 16-4-18	7-1-17 7-8-17	Sick Wounded	Lewis Gun General (1)	9/15. 6/16-5/17	Mention 7.8.17	(2) 9th Jan (E) 16.4.18	—	—	O.T.C. 5 years
Capt	A.W. McDermott	OC B Coy	9.9.14	5.8.15	10.7.15 5-6.16	21.8.17	W'ounded	Gas. Egypt.	11.7.18	Dispatches 21.7.17 (L)		—	—	on leave.
T/Capt	P. Burn	2nd i/c B Coy	3.12.14 (Tem-h)	24.5.17	19.12.15 24.5.17	9/16	Wounded	Signalling Musketry	1915. 1916. 1917	—	(E) 4 - 4.17.	1/12 (7 Leinsters)	a/Sgt. (7 Leinsters)	
T/Capt	G.M. Crawford	OC C Coy	16.4.15	20.8.17	10.7.15.	—	—	—	—	—	(L)	—	—	on leave.
T/Capt	G.J. Hamlet.	OC D Coy	25.4.15	7.2.17	19.8.16	—	—	L.G.	9/16	Dispatches 24.5.18	(L) 2.4.18	—	—	
T/Capt	Q.E. Kemp D.C.M R. Ir. Rifles. (Reg.)	2nd i/c D Coy	19.7.15 (Reg)	30.5.16. Lieut 19.9.17 T/Capt.	13.8.14 4.4.17 present.	13.10.15	Wounded	Musk. Drums. Drill Gas.	12/96. 7/917.	D.C.M. 31.10.14.	(E) 4.4.17	7 7/12 2nd Worcestershire Regt	Sgt. 2nd Worcestershire Regt	
Lieut	W.Y. Beaumont M.C		28.12.15.	1-7-17.	10.7.16	—	—	L. Gun (2) Trench mortars Sniping General	5/16. 5/18 3/16 4/16 4/20 5/16	M.C 7.6.17.	(L) 5-8	9/12 1 Leinster Regt	Pte 1 Leinster Regt	
T/Lieut	E. Clark		9.11.15	1-7-17	26.12.16	—	—	Musk. Drill Bombing Salvo L.G Gas Egypt	2.17. 4.17. 5.17. Sept 16	—	(L)	—	—	on leave.
Lieut	C.W. Kidson		25-5-15.	1-7-17.	28.10.16. 2.7.18	22.4.17	Wounded	Musketry Signalling Bombing General	Sept 16 Feb 16 oct '7 Jany '7	—	(E) 2.7.18	8/12 18 Roy. Jus.	a.c. 18 Roy Ins.	
Lieut	D.R. Lamb Km		24.10.16.	15.4.18	16.11.16 10.11.17	8.4.17	Sick	Musketry L.G. Gas Dublin	7.11.16	—	(E) 10.9.17	—	—	
Lieut	B.P. Blaney		15.12.15	1-7-17.	7.16 2.8.17 19.8.17	23.10.16 7.6.17	Wounded Wounded	Lewis Gun Scouting Sniping Anti Gas	Feb 18 Aug 17	—	(E) 19-8-17	—	—	Immediate O.T.C. June to Dec 15

Officers 2nd Battalion The Royal Dublin Fusiliers

Rank	Name	Date of 1st Appointment Comsn	Date of Present Rank	Service in Present War From	To	Cause of Quitting	Courses Nature	Year	Honours + mentions	Date of Embarkation (E)/Last leave (L)	Service in Ranks Year	Last Rank	Remarks
Lieut	E. Greaves	28.8.15	1.7.17	14.12.15 26.12.16	3.6.16	Wounded	Bombing Lewis gun Trench mortar Gas	1/16 3/16 11/16 4/17 6/17	—	(E) 14.12.16	8/12 7 Leinsters	L.C.	
Lieut	S.E.A. Alcock	22.11.16	22.5.18	5.10.14 17.1.17	1.7.16	fm Comsn	L.gun, M.Artsh, Anti-Gas	Jan 18 —	—	(E) 17.1.17	2 3/12 P.P.C.R.9	Pte	
Lieut	D.C.A. Shepard	27.10.16	27.4.18	29.12.16 2.7.18	27.5.17	wounded	Bombing (3)	16.17.18	—	(E) 2.7.18	—	—	
Lieut	Jws Jones	24.11.15	24.11.15	29.6.17	25.6.18	Sick	—	—	—	(E) 29.6.17	—	—	Hospital
Lieut	G.D. O'Hea	26.9.17	26.9.17	6.4.15 5.2.18	4.4.17	fm Comsn	—	—	—	(E) 5.2.18	2 6/12 A.S.C. — M.T.	Pte	
Lieut	F.A. Walkey	26.4.17	26.4.17	10.7.15 23.6.17 6.3.18	29.11.16 3.8.17	Sw Comsn Wounded	—	—	—	(E) 6.3.18	2 yrs 7 R.D.F.	Pte	
Lieut	S.J. Byrne D.C.M.	26.9.17	26.9.17	4.8.14 16.3.15 2.7.18	23.12.14 20.9.17	fm India fm Comsn	—	—	D.C.M. Oct 15	(E) 2.7.18	7 7/12 R.D.F.	a/C.S.M.	
Lieut	T.P. Nolan	30.5.17	30.5.17	19.8.17	—	—	—	—	—	(E) 19.8.17	2 7/12 R.E.	Sappe	
Lieut	W. Sutherland MM	29.8.17	29.8.17	14.11.15 30.11.17	21.11.16 present	Wounded	Stokes Gun + Trench Warfare	3/1917	Mil. Medal 9/16	(E) 30.11.17	2 8/12	L. Cpl.	Served in Rank of 23rd Ray Fus.
Lieut	P.K. White	1.8.17	1.8.17	1.6.15 1.12.17	12.1.16	Wounded	Drill Musky Malmester	Sept/1916 Aug/16 Sept '16	—	(E) 1.12.17	3 1/2 4/ R.D.F.	Cpl	
Lieut	R. Beeg	24.3.17	24.3.17	14.8.17	24.6.18	Sick	Scouts Egypt	1.11.17	—	(E) 14.8.17	—	—	
2/Lieut	H.C.L. Perrier	29.8.17	29.8.17	5.2.18	—	—	Gas	12/1917	—	—	10/12 3R. D.F.	L.Cpl. D.F.	

Officers 2nd Battalion The Royal Dublin Fusiliers

Rank	Name	Appointment	Date of 1st Commn	Date of Present Rank	Service in Present War From	To	Cause of Quitting	Courses Nature	Year	Honours & Mentions	Date of Embark (1st overseas)	Service in Ranks Years	Last Rank	Remarks
Lieut	S. Morris			20.2.17	Apr 15 March 1·7·13	Oct 15 Aug 17	Wounds	Drill Chelsea Musk Altar M.G. Longman	Jan 14 Dec 17 Apr 68	✓	(E) 1.7.18	17 6/12 Roy Dub Fus	C.S.M.	
Lieut	W. O'Connor		17.3.18	17 3.18	9·7·15	2·7·18	Hosp.	Anti Gas	Aug 17	Serbian Eagle	(E) 9.7.15	7/12 Connaught Rgrs	C.S.M.	Hospl.
Lieut	A.H. Philmer		17.6.17	17.6.17	19·8·17	–	✓	Gas Dublin Bomb Harret Gas France	Aug 17 Dec 17 June 18	–	(E) 14.8.17	–	–	
Lieut	J.W. Elvery		25.6.17	25 6·17	10·7·15 30·11·17	10·12·16	Commn	Trench warfare	Apr 18	–	(E) 30·11·17	2 7/12 7 R.D.F.	L Sgt	
Lieut	E.A. Poulter		26.4.17	26·4·17	10·7·15 16·6·17 6·3·18	3·4·16 9·8·17	Sick (Wounded)	Musk A ShP	Jan 18	–	(E) 6·3·18	2 7/12 7 R. Dub Fus	Cpl	
Lieut	G.H. McElvany		3·7·	3·7·15	1·7·17 14·2·17	15·5·16 9·9·16	Wounded	Musketry Bombing	Apr 16 Mar 16	–	(E) 14·2·17	–	–	
Lieut	H.W. Waghorn R.W.K. Regt		14·4·15	1·7·17 30·9·15	–	–	–	Bombing L. Gun Anti Gas	17·12·16 13·4·17 2·4·17	–	(L) 6·7·18	–	–	on leave

W.M Welton Lieut. Colonel,

Demog. 2nd Battn. Royal Dublin Fusrs.

(6339) Wt. W160/M3016 1,500,000 10/17 McA & W Ltd (E 1898) Forms W3091. Army Form W.3091.

Cover for Documents.

Nature of Enclosures.

CONFIDENTIAL

War Diary
of
2nd Bn. ROYAL DUBLIN FUSILIERS
from
1 December 1918
to
31 December 1918

Vol No 53

Notes, or Letters written.

2nd Batt. Royal Dublin Fusiliers   Sheet 1

Army Form C. 2118.

WAR DIARY
or
INTELLIGENCE SUMMARY.
(Erase heading not required.)

Instructions regarding War Diaries and Intelligence Summaries are contained in F. S. Regs., Part II. and the Staff Manual respectively. Title pages will be prepared in manuscript.

Place	Date	Hour	Summary of Events and Information	Remarks and references to Appendices
BAS LIEU	1st Decr 1918		R.C. Service in AVESNES Church at 8am. His Majesty the King accompanied by the Prince of Wales (Prince Albert) with his Staff saw the Battalion & troops of 50th Division in a field off the MAUBERGE-AVESNES Road at 11-30am. Training & Educational Classes continued. Lecture to Batt. by Dr Alexander Irvine at 2-15pm. G.O.C. Brigade present.	
	2nd Decr 1918			
	3rd Decr 1918		Training & Educational Classes continued. Major A.J. MacDermott arrived.	
	4th Decr 1918		Training & Educational Classes continued.	
	5th Decr 1918		The Battalion left BAS LIEU at 9-30am arrived in MONCEAU ST WAAST about 11-30am	
MONCEAU ST WAAST	6th Decr 1918		Educational classes continued. C.O. inspected Batt. in marching order after which the Batt. was re-organised to meet the new conditions required by Educational Scheme and impending demobilization. A & D Coys were formed of those with trades or callings before enlistment whose re-employment on return to civil life is already assured. B Coy took all serving soldiers (men attending school). C Coy took men with out trades or callings who have no jobs to go to on return to civil life, men learning trades in the Battalion shops, also those desirous of learning trades outside the Batt., such as motoring, Electric lighting, engineering etc.	
	7th Decr 1918		Training & Educational Classes. Lectures on Flying, Football	

2nd Batt. Royal Dublin Fusiliers Sheet 2

Army Form C. 2118.

WAR DIARY
or
INTELLIGENCE SUMMARY.
(Erase heading not required.)

Instructions regarding War Diaries and Intelligence Summaries are contained in F. S. Regs., Part II. and the Staff Manual respectively. Title pages will be prepared in manuscript.

Place	Date	Hour	Summary of Events and Information	Remarks and references to Appendices
MONCEAU ST WAAST	8-12-18		Church Parade.	
	9-12-18		Training parades roetad. Brigadier inspected draft of 40 O.R. recently joined men	
	10-12-18		Training parades roetad as usual. Lt WALMSLEY R.A.F. delivered a lecture on Flying	
	11-12-18		Lt COUGHLAN's Lecture to Bn "A WORD ON THE COLONIES"	
	12-12-18		" "	
	13-12-18		" "	
	14-12-18		Training & cross country Run. Ro school	
	15-12-18		Church parade	
	16-12-18		Training & cross country run. Educational Training. The Corps Commander Sir. C.K.R. Morland K.C.B. K.C.M.G. D.S.O. Commanding XIII Corps visited the Batt. & inspected billets.	
	17-12-18		advance party sent to LE QUESNOY.	
	18-12-18		Training & school as usual.	
	19-12-18		Battalion marched from MONCEAU ST WAAST to LE QUESNOY	
	20-12-18		Cleaning billets.	
LE QUESNOY			Cleaning & repairing billets. Major A.J. MacDermot takes over duties of Town Major J LE QUESNOY	
	21-12-18		Church parade	
	22-12-18		Cleaning area & repairing billets. Intimation of award of V.C. to Sergt Curtis received from Brigade.	

2nd Battn. Royal Dublin Fusiliers Sheet 3

Army Form C. 2118.

WAR DIARY
or
INTELLIGENCE SUMMARY.
(Erase heading not required.)

Instructions regarding War Diaries and Intelligence Summaries are contained in F. S. Regs., Part II. and the Staff Manual respectively. Title pages will be prepared in manuscript.

Place	Date	Hour	Summary of Events and Information	Remarks and references to Appendices
LE QUESNOY	24.12.-	18	Brigade parades for presentation of Medal Ribbons by Divisional Commander Sergt. Curtis receives the Ribbon of the V.C.	
	25.12.	18	Church Parade	
	26.12.	18	Holiday	
	27.12.	18	Drill parades, cleaning Battalion Area	
	28.12.	18	Drill parades	
	29.12.	18	Church Parade	
	30.12.	18	School re-opens. 2 Companies salvage	
	31.12.	17	School. 2 Companies on salvage. Drill parade 3pm to 4pm.	

Effective Strength - Officers   34
                         do   - O-Ranks   718
                     Ration Sgth Officers   28
                        do   do O-Ranks   600

2nd Batt. Royal Dublin Fusiliers   Sheet 4.

Army Form C. 2118.

WAR DIARY
or
INTELLIGENCE SUMMARY.
(Erase heading not required.)

Instructions regarding War Diaries and Intelligence Summaries are contained in F. S. Regs., Part II. and the Staff Manual respectively. Title pages will be prepared in manuscript.

Place	Date	Hour	Summary of Events and Information	Remarks and references to Appendices
			Awards for gallantry in the Field during Operations in November be were granted to the undermentioned of the Battalion	
Bar to M.C.			2/Lieut. L. A. Morris M.C.	
M.C.			Capt (Rev) J.J. Delaney C.F.	
			Capt. F. M. Kiernan	
			Lieut. E. Greaves. (Deceased)	
D.C.M.			10090 Sgt Gaynor F	
			26813 L/Cpl Connero P	
			15829 Pte Starkie J.	
Bar to D.C.M.			15834 Sgt Perry F	
			27980 " Green W.	
V.C.			14017 Sgt Curtis H. A.	

R McRae Kerr Lt
& Adjutant
2nd Bn. Royal Dublin Fusiliers.

(6392) Wt. W6192/P875 1,500,000 4/18 McA & W Ltd (E 2815) Forms W3091/4.   Army Form W.3091.

Cover for Documents.

Nature of Enclosures.

Confidential

War Diary
of
2nd Battalion The Royal Dublin Fusiliers
From 1st January 1919
To 31st January 1919.

Vol. No 54.

Notes, or Letters written,

Army Form C. 2118.

WAR DIARY
or
INTELLIGENCE SUMMARY.
(Erase heading not required.)

Instructions regarding War Diaries and Intelligence Summaries are contained in F. S. Regs. Part II. and the Staff Manual respectively. Title pages will be prepared in manuscript.

Place	Date	Hour	Summary of Events and Information	Remarks and references to Appendices
Le Quesnoy	1-1-19		Rehearsals for "Trooping" and "Colours"	
	2-1-19		"Taking over of Colours" took place on the Parade ground in the Barracks at 11.00 hrs. Divisional Commander and Brigadier were present.	
	3-1-19		3 Coys on salvage. School resumed.	
	4-1-19		3 Coys on salvage. Classes carried on.	10 O.R. Demobilized
	5-1-19		Church Parade. Lecture in theatre in evening by ___	
	6-1-19		2 Coys on salvage. School.	
	7-1-19.		1 Coy on salvage. One Coy reorganization school.	3 O.R. Demobilized
	8-1-19.		Holiday.	
	9-1-19		Baths in afternoon.	
	10-1-19		2 Coys salvage. School. Corps Commander inspected Barracks.	
	11-1-19		1 Coy salvage. School.	
	12-1-19.		Church Parade.	
	13-1-19.		2 Coys salvage. School.	1 officer 10 O.R. Demobilized
	14-1-19.		School. Lecture in Barrack Rooms. No salvage owing to weather	2 O.R. Demobilized
	15-1-19.		1 Coy salvage. School.	
	16-1-19.		1 Coy salvage. Battalion had baths in afternoon.	

WAR DIARY or INTELLIGENCE SUMMARY.

Army Form C. 2118.

Place	Date	Hour	Summary of Events and Information	Remarks and references to Appendices
LE QUESNOY	17-1-19		1 Coy. Salvage. School.	5.O.R. Demobilized
	18-1-19		Church Parade.	
	19-1-19		1 Coy. Salvage. School.	
	20-1-19		1 Coy. Salvage. School.	2 Officers & 33 O.R. Demobilized
	21-1-19		1 Coy. Salvage. School.	Divisional General visited Barracks and school
	22-1-19		1 Coy. Salvage. School.	4.O.R. Demobilized
	23-1-19		1 Coy. Salvage. School.	
	24-1-19		1 Coy. Salvage. School.	
	25-1-19		1 Coy. Salvage. School.	4.O.R. Demobilized
	26-1-19		Church Parade.	3.O.R. Demobilized
	27-1-19		1 Coy. Salvage. School.	
	28-1-19		No Salvage owing to weather (snow) Route march. School. Brig. Genl. 149 Bde. visited Btn.	1 Officer & 39 O.R. Demobilized
	29-1-19		No Salvage owing to snow & frost. Route march. Brig. Genl. 149 Bde. inspect transport line.	4. O.R. Demobilized
	30-1-19		No Salvage owing to snow & frost. Route march. School.	
	31-1-19		No Salvage owing to snow on ground. Route march. School.	

(6392) Wt. W6192/P875 1,500,000 4/18 McA & W Ltd (E 2815) Forms W3091/4.   Army Form W.3091.

Cover for Documents.

Nature of Enclosures.

Confidential
War Diary
of
2 Batt. The Royal Dublin Fus.⁵
from 1ˢᵗ February 1919
to   28ᵗʰ   "   1919.

Vol no. 54

Notes, or Letters written.

Army Form C. 2118.

Vol. No 54

WAR DIARY
or
INTELLIGENCE SUMMARY.
(Erase heading not required.)

Instructions regarding War Diaries and Intelligence Summaries are contained in F. S. Regs., Part II. and the Staff Manual respectively. Title pages will be prepared in manuscript.

Place	Date	Hour	Summary of Events and Information	Remarks and references to Appendices
LE QUESNOY	Feby 1st/19		Cavalry turn out and foot salvage work was not carried out. Boys played games in forenoon. B Coy attended school	
"	2-2-19		Church Parade	
"	3-2-19		Boy Parade and B Coy School	
"	4-2-19		Boys played games. Indoor Drill and School	
"	5-2-19		B Coy School. Boys Parade	
"	6-2-19		B Coy School. Boys Parade	
"	7-2-19		Snow and frost continue. No salvage work. Boys Parade. B Coy School	
"	8-2-19		Church Parade	
"	9-2-19		B Coy School. Boys Parade	
"	10-2-19		Boys cleaning streets. Baths	
"	11-2-19		Return draft Parade. "B" Boys School	
"	12-2-19		Boys street cleaning. B Coy School	
"	13-2-19		Boys played games. Street clearing. "B" Boys School	
"	14-2-19		Boys Gymnasium. B Coy School. Street clearing	
"	15-2-19		Return draft Parade for inspection by Brig Genl. 149th Bde. Coy Gymnasium. Street clearing. 9 men Demobilized	
"	16-2-19		Return draft drill Parade. B Coy School	
"	17-2-19		Church Parade	
"	18-2-19		Draft Parade. B Coy School	
"	19-2-19		" " " "	
"	20-2-19		" " " street clearing	
"	21-2-19		" " " "	

Lieut. Colonel.
Comdg. 2nd Battn. Royal Dublin Fusrs.

Army Form C. 2118.

WAR DIARY
or
INTELLIGENCE SUMMARY.
(Erase heading not required.)

Place	Date	Hour	Summary of Events and Information	Remarks and references to Appendices
LE QUESNOY	Feb 22/19		Battalion Rest Day. Preliminary Examination for 2nd 3rd Class Certificates (A.E.)	
"	23.2.19		Church Parade	
"	24.2.19		Drill Parade	
"	25.2.19		" "	
"	26.2.19		" "	
"	27.2.19		Khaki draft (16.1st/Bn) paraded for inspection by Genl. Division at 1.45 pm and entrained at 2.30 pm.	
"	28.2.19		Battalion reorganized into one Coy.	

Signature (illegible)

(6392) Wt. W6192/P875 1,500,000 4/18 McA & W Ltd (E 2815) Forms W3091/4.

Army Form W.3091.

Cover for Documents.

Nature of Enclosures.

Confidental

War Diary of 2nd Battalion The Royal Dublin Fusiliers

For the month of March 1919

Volume number 55

Notes, or Letters written.

Army Form C. 2118.

Vol 55

WAR DIARY
or
INTELLIGENCE SUMMARY.
(Erase heading not required.)

Instructions regarding War Diaries and Intelligence Summaries are contained in F. S. Regs., Part II. and the Staff Manual respectively. Title pages will be prepared in manuscript.

Place	Date	Hour	Summary of Events and Information	Remarks and references to Appendices
Le Quesnoy	1.3.19		Drill parade. School.	
"	2.3.19		Church parade	
"	3.3.19		Drill parade cleaning streets School	
"	4.3.19		" " " "	
"	5.3.19		" " " "	
"	6.3.19		" " " "	
"	7.3.19		" " " "	
"	8.3.19		" " " "	
"	9.3.19		" " " "	
"	10.3.19		" " " "	
"	11.3.19		" " " "	
"	12.3.19		" " " "	
"	13.3.19		Battalion warned to proceed to England on Cadre on 17th	
"	14.3.19		Stores collected 3/R. Dus made up deficiencies from our stores	
"	15.3.19		Commander in Chief visits Division Preparation made for going away	
"	16.3.19		Wires for hose of the Cadre cancelled. Church parade	

J Grah[?]
Lieut Colonel
Detach. 2nd Batt. Royal Dublin Fus[iliers]

Army Form C. 2118.

Vol 55

WAR DIARY
or
INTELLIGENCE SUMMARY.
(Erase heading not required.)

Instructions regarding War Diaries and Intelligence Summaries are contained in F. S. Regs., Part II. and the Staff Manual respectively. Title pages will be prepared in manuscript.

Place	Date	Hour	Summary of Events and Information	Remarks and references to Appendices
Le Quesnoy	17.3.19		St Patricks Day Church Parade Dance for men in the evening whole holiday	
"	18.3.19		Battalion moves from Barracks into Billets (Le Quesnoy)	
"	19.3.19		School for Band. Duty for remainder of Battalion	
"	20.3.19		" " " "	
"	21.3.19		" " " "	
"	22.3.19		" " " "	
"	23.3.19		Church Parade. Band Concert in the evening	
"	24.3.19		School for Band. Duty for remainder of Battalion	
"	25.3.19		" " " "	
"	26.3.19		" " " "	
"	27.3.19		3 Guns Captured by N.J. Division presented to Town Le Quesnoy by Brigadier General. P.C.M. Robinson Officers and Band present.	
"	28.3.19		Band Practice	
"	29.3.19		Band practice clearing snow from vicinity of Billets	
"	30.3.19		Church Parade Band Concert in evening	
"	31.3.19		Band practice, Demobilization having proceeded at varying rates since November 1918 the Battalion is now reduced to a ration strength of 11 Officers & 50 Other Ranks, with Officers 4 and 117 Other Ranks on Command.	

(6392) Wt. W6192/P875 1,500,000 4/18 McA & W Ltd (E 2815) Forms W3091/4.   Army Form W.3091.

Cover for Documents.

Nature of Enclosures.

Confidential
War Diary
of
2nd Battalion The Royal Dublin Fusiliers
From 1st April 1919.
To 30th April 1919.

Volume No 57.

Notes, or Letters written.

Army Form C. 2118.

Vol. No 57

WAR DIARY
or
INTELLIGENCE SUMMARY.
(Erase heading not required.)

Instructions regarding War Diaries and Intelligence Summaries are contained in F. S. Regs., Part II. and the Staff Manual respectively. Title pages will be prepared in manuscript.

Place	Date	Hour	Summary of Events and Information	Remarks and references to Appendices
IN QUARTERS	1919. April 1st to 5th		Usual practice and School daily.	
	6th		Church Parades. Cadre and Band of 1st Battalion arrive in Chester.	
	7th, 8th, 9th		Band Practice and School daily	
	10th		" " " Battalion receive Gild's Inspection.	
	11th		" " "	
	12th		Bands Practice.	
	13th		Band Practice and School Cadre at Inspection on 10th.	
	14th to		Church Parades. Massed Bands of 2nd Leinsters, 10th & 1st Bn. Royal Dublin Fusiliers	
	19th		played selections on the Place D'Armes on Easter Monday (21st)	
	20th		Band Practice and School daily. Marching order parade on 24th.	
	21st to		Church Parades.	
	27th		Band Practice and School daily.	
	28th to			
	30th			

[signature] Bramfor
Lieut. Colonel.
Commdg, 2nd Battn. Royal Dublin Fusrs.

www.ingramcontent.com/pod-product-compliance
Lightning Source LLC
Chambersburg PA
CBHW081451160426
43193CB00013B/2443